MUMMIES
and Ancient Egypt

GARETH STEVENS
GS
PUBLISHING
A Member of the WRC Media Family of Companies

by Anita Ganeri
Consultant: Dr. Anne Millard

First published in 2005 by
Gareth Stevens Publishing
A WRC Media Company
330 West Olive Street, Suite 100
Milwaukee, Wisconsin 53212 USA

ISBN 0-8368-6290-2

This U.S. edition copyright © 2005 by Gareth Stevens, Inc.

Original edition copyright © 2004 by ticktock Entertainment Ltd.
First published in Great Britain in 2005 by ticktock Media Ltd.,
Unit 2, Orchard Business Centre, North Farm Road, Tunbridge
Wells, Kent, TN2 3XF, United Kingdom.

Gareth Stevens series editor: Dorothy L. Gibbs
Gareth Stevens art direction and cover design: Tammy West

Picture credits (t=top, b=bottom, c=center, l=left, r=right)
The Ancient Egypt Picture Library: 21 br. Art Archive: 5l, 5br,
7tr, 9tr, 13tr, 15tl, 17tr, 18-19b, 19cl, 19cr, 22-23. British
Museum: 7cr, 9cr, 11tr, 11cr, 13br, 16, 17br. Corbis: 5tr, 7br,
10-11, 11tl, 14-15, 15br, 21l. Egyptian Museum, Berlin: 1, 6bl,
9bl, 12-13, 19tl. Egyptian Museum, Cairo: 2-3, 6-7, 7tl, 9tl,
9br, 11br, 13cr, 15tr, 15cr, 18l, 19tr. Louvre Museum, Paris: 20,
22bl, 23tr. Science Photo Library: 8-9. Werner Forman: 17l,
19br, 21tr.

Every effort has been made to trace the copyright holders for the
photos used in this book. The publisher apologizes, in advance, for
any unintentional omissions and would be pleased to insert appropriate
acknowledgments in any subsequent edition of this publication.

Printed in China

1 2 3 4 5 6 7 8 9 09 08 07 06 05

Contents

Words in the glossary
are printed in **boldface**
type the first time they
appear in the text.

A Kingdom on the Nile River

More than five thousand years ago, people living along the banks of the Nile River, in Egypt, built a rich and powerful kingdom. This kingdom, known as **ancient** Egypt, lasted thousands of years.

Map of Egypt and the Nile River.

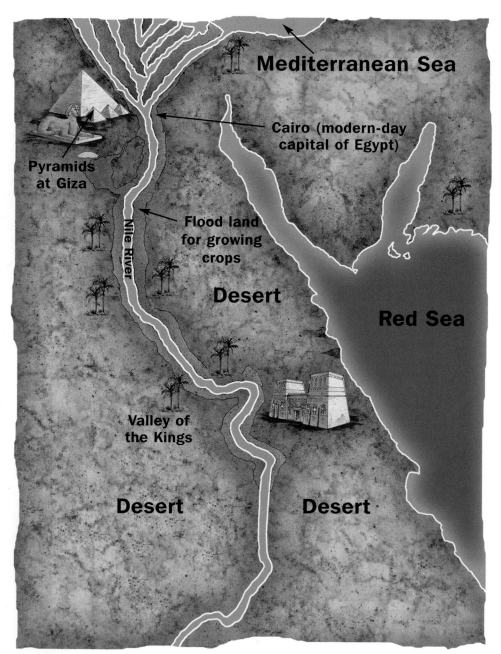

Mediterranean Sea

Cairo (modern-day capital of Egypt)

Pyramids at Giza

Nile River

Flood land for growing crops

Desert

Red Sea

Valley of the Kings

Desert

Desert

Egypt is very hot and dry, with sandy and rocky deserts on both sides of the Nile. Every year, for hundreds of years, the Nile River flooded, making lots of mud that piled up along its banks. The rich, muddy soil was perfect for growing crops. Today, flooding in the Nile Valley is more controlled.

The people of ancient Egypt used the Nile River for growing food and for traveling around. Because travel on land was very difficult, boats carried people and goods up and down the river. The first Egyptian boats were made out of **reeds**. Later, wood was used instead.

Model of an ancient Egyptian boat.

Egyptian Artifacts

People today know a lot about ancient Egypt because of the **artifacts** Egyptians left behind.

In ancient Egypt, pictures called hieroglyphs were used to write things down.

The ancient Egyptians were brilliant at making mummies!

Amazing Mummi s

A mummy is a dead body that has been **embalmed** and wrapped in bandages to **preserve** it for thousands of years. The ancient Egyptians believed that dead people went to live in another world, where their bodies were still needed. To keep dead bodies from rotting, the Egyptians made them into mummies.

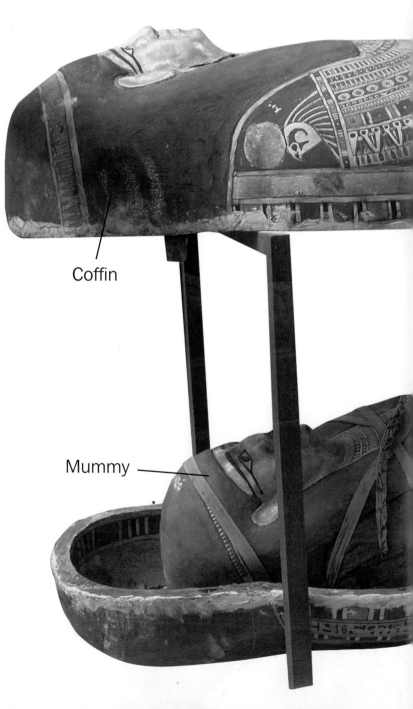

Some mummies were placed in beautiful **coffins**, decorated with gold and precious gems. Often, a golden mask covered the mummy's face.

Coffin

Mask

Mummy

A mummy's coffin was sometimes placed inside a stone chest called a sarcophagus.

The ancient Egyptians made animal mummies, too. This mummy is a pet cat.

Many Egyptian mummies still exist today. They are usually found in museums.

This mummy is an ibis. Ibis are waterbirds that were sacred to the ancient Egyptians.

A crocodile mummy was a **symbol** of the crocodile god, Sobek. The Egyptians believed that Sobek controlled the waters of the Nile River.

7

Making a Mummy

The men in charge of making mummies were called embalmers. The chief embalmer wore a **jackal** mask. The jackal was the special animal of embalmers.

To make a mummy, embalmers first washed the dead body. Next, they took out the body's insides. The brain was pulled out through the nose! They put the insides into four special jars, then rubbed the body with oil and wrapped it in bandages.

When a mummy was placed in its coffin, piles of salt were packed around the body to dry it out, and the body was stuffed with sawdust or rags and **herbs**.

A golden coffin.

Anubis, who was the god of embalmers, was pictured with a jackal's head.

Good luck charms, such as this **scarab**, were tucked between a mummy's bandages.

Egyptians believed that a magic eye protected mummies in the **next world**.

Four **canopic jars** held the lungs, liver, stomach, and intestines of a mummy's dead body.

Gods and Temples

In ancient Egypt, people worshiped hundreds of gods and goddesses. They believed that their gods created the world and looked after it. In ancient pictures, many Egyptian gods are shown with animal heads.

The people of ancient Egypt built great **temples** as homes for their gods. The temples were very important places. Only **priests** could go inside. Ordinary people had to stay outside.

An ancient Egyptian painting of a priest.

A statue of a god stood inside each temple. A priest dressed and fed the statue because the ancient Egyptians believed the god's **spirit** lived inside the statue. Egyptian priests also said prayers and made **offerings** to the gods.

An ancient temple in Egypt.

This statue is Ra. He was the god of the Sun, who Egyptians believed created the world.

Osiris was the god of the dead. He married Isis, the goddess of women.

Horus, the son of Isis and Osiris, was the sky god. He is often pictured with a **falcon**'s head.

The Pharaoh

The king of Egypt was called the pharaoh. As the most powerful person in the whole country, he was in charge of all the land and all the people.

The pharaoh lived in great **luxury** in a palace. He sat on a throne in the great hall of the palace to carry out his royal duties.

People thought the pharaoh was a living god. They came from all over Egypt to ask him to solve their problems and settle their arguments. On special occasions, the pharaoh wore a crown and a false beard.

Although Queen Hatshepsut was a woman pharaoh, she still had to wear a false beard.

Tutankhamun was only nine years old when he became Egypt's pharaoh.

Ramesses the Great was a brave Egyptian soldier who built many temples and statues.

Pyramids and Tombs

When the first Egyptian pharaohs died, their mummies were placed inside pyramids, which were gigantic stone **tombs** with sloping sides. Some pyramids are still standing!

The pharaohs were buried with magnificent treasures to take with them into the next world, but tomb robbers broke into many of the pyramids and stole the treasures!

Later in history, mummies and their treasures were hidden in tombs cut deep into rocky cliffs, but even these tombs were not safe from robbers.

An uncovered tomb in the
Valley of the Kings.

The Great Pyramid at Giza is the
biggest pyramid of all. It is made
up of more than two million
huge stone blocks and
took thousands of
workers more than
twenty years
to build.

Tutankhamun's Tomb

Archaeologists found
treasures, such as this
pendant, in Pharaoh
Tutankhamun's tomb.

This beautiful bracelet
is decorated with
scarab beetles.

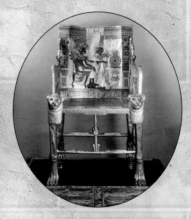

Tutankhamun's golden
throne is covered with
precious gems.

Egyptians at Home

Most houses in ancient Egypt were built using bricks made of dried mud. **Wealthy** Egyptians had large houses with gardens. Poor families lived in smaller houses that had only one room. That room was the family's living room, dining room, and bedroom!

This clay model of a poor Egyptian's house was found in a tomb. On hot nights, people slept outside on the roof to keep cool.

The ancient Egyptians ate meat, fish, vegetables, and fruit. They also ate a lot of tough, gritty bread, which they made from wheat and **barley**.

Ancient food has actually been found in Egyptian tombs!

An ancient painting showing Egyptians making bread and beer.

These loaves of bread are 3,500 years old.

Egyptians mashed up bread to make beer. Sometimes, they drank the beer through a straw to **strain** out the lumps!

These **dates** are more than three thousand years old. Egyptians ate dates fresh or dried.

Egyptian Fashion

Clothing that was lightweight and loose-fitting kept the ancient Egyptians cool in their hot, desert **climate**. Most of their clothing was made of **linen**.

Egyptian men often wore short skirts. They were made from a piece of linen that was wrapped around the waist and tied with a knot. Sometimes, the men also wore **cloaks**.

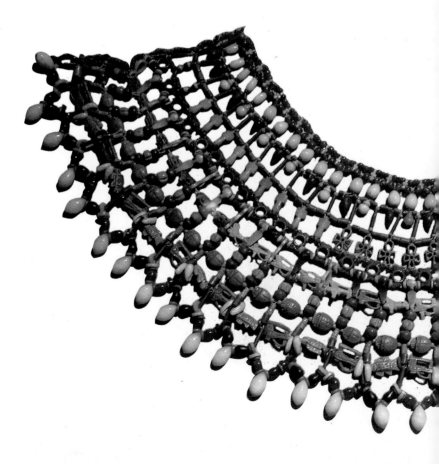

Egyptian women wore long, linen dresses with linen **shawls**. The dresses often had **pleats** and were decorated with beads. Both men and women in ancient Egypt wore makeup and jewelry.

This Egyptian necklace is made up of thousands of tiny beads.

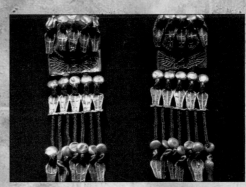

Earrings were made from gold and gems such as garnet, turquoise, and **lapis lazuli**.

Most of the time, Egyptians went barefoot, but, sometimes, they wore sandals made out of reeds.

Many women in ancient Egypt wore wigs.

School Days

Most of the children in ancient Egypt did not go to school. Girls helped their mothers at home. Boys worked with their fathers. Some boys from wealthy families went to schools run by temple priests.

At school, the teachers were very strict, and lazy students were harshly punished.

Instead of alphabet letters, Egyptian writing used pictures called hieroglyphs. Each picture stood for a word or a sound. Egyptian boys learned how to read by **chanting** long lists of hieroglyphs out loud.

Ancient Egyptian hieroglyphs.

Egyptian boys practiced writing on pieces of wood or broken stone and clay.

Some students became writers called scribes. Their training took many years, but it prepared them for good jobs. They kept records for the pharaoh and his kingdom.

An Egyptian scribe.

Egyptian children had lots of toys, such as this little dog — which has a mouth that moves!

Egyptians at Work

Some ancient Egyptians were temple priests, others worked for the pharaoh as scribes, but most Egyptians were farmers or builders.

When the Nile River flooded, farmers could not work in the fields, so they took turns working for the pharaoh, building new temples, pyramids, and tombs.

Each November, after the flood waters had gone down, farmers plowed their fields and planted seeds. In March or April, they harvested crops.

A model of an Egyptian farmer plowing.

Egyptian farmers dug small ditches around their fields and filled them with water from the Nile. They used **shadufs** to pull up water from the river.

Some people still use shadufs today. The person in this picture is using a shaduf.

Egyptian Artifacts

Ancient Egyptian artists and craftspeople made jewelry, pots, and baskets.

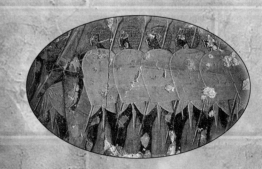

Some of the men in ancient Egypt learned to fight and became soldiers in the Egyptian army.

Glossary

ancient: from a time early in history

archaeologists (ar-kee-AH-luh-gists): people who dig for objects that help them study history

artifacts: items, such as tools and decorative ornaments, made by people

barley: a type of grain

canopic jars (keh-NO-pic jars): special containers used to preserve the insides of dead people

chanting: singing in one repeated tone

climate: the normal weather of a place

cloaks: sleeveless coats, or capes

coffins: the large, boxlike containers in which dead bodies are buried

dates: the sweet fruits of palm trees

embalmed (im-BAHMD): treated with chemicals to prevent decaying, or rotting

falcon: a large, hawklike hunting bird

herbs: sweet-smelling plants that are often used to make medicines

jackal: a wild dog with large ears

lapis lazuli (LAP-iss LAZ-uh-lee): a blue gemstone

linen: cloth made from the fibers of the flax plant

luxury: a state of wealth and comfort

next world: the place where the ancient Egyptians believed people's spirits went after their bodies died

offerings: gifts from people to gods

pendant: a type of necklace that is usually a charm hanging from a chain

pleats: fanlike folds in cloth

preserve: to keep something in its original form or condition

priests: people who carry out special duties in a church or a temple

reeds: plants with long, strong stems, or stalks, that grow in marshes and along riverbanks

scarab (SCARE-ub): a beetle that the ancient Egyptians thought was lucky

shadufs (shah-DOOFS): very simple, hand-operated machines used to lift water out of rivers

shawls: long, wide scarves worn over the shoulders

spirit: an unseen life force

strain: (v) to pass through small holes, separating solids from liquids

symbol: an object or figure that stands for something else

temples: buildings where people go to pray and worship

tombs: places where dead bodies are buried

wealthy: having a lot of money and valuable possessions